My family cele...
Hanukkah

Cath Senker

Photography by Chris Fairclough

W
FRANKLIN WATTS

First published in 2009 by
Franklin Watts. This edition 2013
338 Euston Road
London NW1 3BH

Franklin Watts Australia
Level 17/207 Kent Street
Sydney NSW 2000

ISBN: 978 1 4451 1935 9

Dewey classification number: 296.4'35

A CIP catalogue record for this book is available
from the British Library.

Planning and production by Discovery Books Limited
Editor: Laura Durman
Designer: Ian Winton
Photography by Chris Fairclough

The author and photographer would like to acknowledge the following for their help in preparing
this book: Sarah, Martin, Emma and Joshua Williams; Guy and Alex Punja; Rabbi Elizabeth Tikvah
Sarah and the congregation of Brighton and Hove Progressive Synagogue, -in particular: Prue
Baker; Jerome Cox-Strong; Susan Kingsley; Sam Kingsley Fried; Sam Whatling.

Please note, the way that people celebrate festivals varies and this book represents the experience
of one family. It should not be assumed that everyone celebrates in the same way.

Printed in China

Franklin Watts is a division of Hachette Children's Books, an Hachette UK company.
www.hachette.co.uk

Words that appear in **bold** in the text are explained in the glossary.

Contents

Globe panels

People celebrate Hanukkah in lots of different ways around the world. Look out for the globe panels for some examples.

About my family and me

My name is Joshua and I'm eight. My sister Emma is 11. I like playing the guitar and drawing cartoons. I'm learning the Korean **martial art** Soo Bahk Do. My sister plays the cello and the piano and goes to drama classes.

Here I am with Emma and Mum and Dad outside our house.

I practise the Soo Bahk Do moves at home.

We're a Jewish family. We carry out the Jewish **customs** at home. Each week, we go to **synagogue** and **religion school**.

My favourite Jewish festival is **Hanukkah**. This book will show you how my family celebrates Hanukkah.

The festival of Hanukkah

At Hanukkah we celebrate an important event in Jewish history. More than 2,000 years ago, the Jewish people fought against the Greek-Syrian army that ruled **ancient Israel**. They took back the city of Jerusalem, including their holy **Temple**.

Emma and I read about the brave Jewish fighters called the **Maccabees**.

It was important to the Jewish people that the **oil lamp** in the Temple was always burning. The Jewish fighters relit the lamp. There was only enough oil to last for one day. But by a miracle it lasted for eight days. By this time, the Jewish people had found more oil.

To remember this miracle, we light candles on a special holder called a **hanukiah**.

We make decorations that remind us of the Hanukkah story.

Lighting the candles

Hanukkah lasts for eight days. On the first day, at nightfall, we light one candle on the hanukiah using the 'helper' candle. On the second day, we light two candles, and on the third day, three. On the last evening we light all eight candles. We say Hanukkah **blessings**.

Emma and I each have our own hanukiah to light.

Mum and Dad place the **hanukiot** by the window. This is to remind people who walk past about the miracle.

We place the hanukiot in the window where our friends and neighbours will see it.

Morocco

In Morocco, Jewish people light the candles on the hanukiah differently. They use a match to light the eight candles, and then light the helper candle last.

Songs and games

After lighting the candles, we sing songs, such as 'Maoz Tzur'. The song tells of the many times in history that the Jewish people were saved from danger.

We play 'Maoz Tzur' on the cello, guitar and trombone. Mum sings the tune.

We play a game with a **dreidel** and tokens. The dreidel has four sides, with the Hebrew letters nun, shin, hay and gimel. The letters stand for the words 'A great miracle happened there'. ('There' means Israel.)

Our family plays like this. We start with 10 tokens each. We all put one token in the pot in the middle. The players spin the dreidel in turn. When it lands on:

Nun: do nothing.

Shin: put all your tokens in the pot.

Hay: take half of the tokens from the pot.

Gimel: take all the tokens from the pot. Everyone else puts one in the pot.

The game ends when one person has won all of the tokens in the game.

I love playing the dreidel game at Hanukkah.

Hanukkah foods

At Hanukkah, we make foods fried in oil. It helps us to remember the miracle of the oil that lasted for eight days in the Temple.

At dinner, we wish each other a Happy Hanukkah.

My favourite dish is potato pancakes called latkes. They are made with grated potato and onions. We often eat them with apple sauce and sour cream. Doughnuts are also popular.

I eat as many latkes as I can. I love them!

Israel

In Israel, the favourite Hanukkah treat is sufganiot. These are doughnuts, filled with jam and fried in oil. In the weeks before Hanukkah, bakers around the country fry hundreds of sufganiot every day.

Gifts and gelt

During the festival, parents offer Hanukkah **gelt** to their children. 'Gelt' is the **Yiddish** word for money. In the past, the gift was a reward for learning the story of Hanukkah well.

USA

In the United States, Jewish parents often give chocolate gelt to their children. Sometimes, families play the dreidel game with chocolate coins as tokens.

My parents sometimes give us chocolate gelt at Hanukkah.

At Hanukkah, many Jewish parents give their children a present. Some give their children a small gift on each day of Hanukkah.

We open our presents. Emma has a special notebook. I have a fantastic book that shows how to draw cartoons.

Hanukkah in the synagogue

At the end of **Shabbat** during Hanukkah, we go to the synagogue to celebrate with other Jewish people. We dress in our best clothes and leave the house at sunset.

First, **Rabbi** Elli leads the **Havdalah** ceremony. We say 'goodbye' to Shabbat and wish each other a happy week.

Lighting the Havdalah candle marks the end of Shabbat and the start of a new week.

Then the children light the candles on the hanukiot. Rabbi Elli asks us to think of a wish for each candle. We hope for health, peace in the **Middle East** and peace in our community.

Rabbi Elli says the Hanukkah lights carry our hopes for a better world.

Hanukkah party

After the service, we have a Hannukah party. People have brought popular Jewish dishes for us to eat, as well as Hanukkah latkes and doughnuts.

There is plenty of food to share.

We eat salads, **bagels** with smoked salmon (middle) and **falafel** (bottom left).

Argentina

In Buenos Aires, the capital of Argentina, there is a big outdoor Hanukkah party. After the lighting of a large hanukiah, a Jewish **klezmer** band plays lively music. People enjoy tasty **kosher** hamburgers and sausages.

The children have a doughnut-eating contest. The doughnuts are hung from the ceiling. We all try to eat our doughnut as quickly as we can. The lucky winner gets a bag of chocolate gelt.

Eating a doughnut in the air is harder than you think!

A Hanukkah recipe: latkes

Why not try this delicious Hanukkah recipe? You can help to make the latkes but please ask an adult to fry them.

You will need
- 4 large potatoes, peeled
- 1 medium-sized onion
- 1 large egg
- 1 teaspoon salt
- $1/2$ teaspoon white pepper
- 1 tablespoon plain flour
- $1/2$ teaspoon baking powder
- vegetable oil (for frying)

1. Grate the potatoes and onion. Put them in a colander. Squeeze the mixture to press out as much liquid as possible.

2. In a large bowl, mix the egg, salt, pepper, flour and baking powder. Add the potato and onion, and mix well.

3. Heat some oil in a frying pan.

4. Drop about 2 tablespoons of potato mixture into the pan for each latke. Flatten the latkes with the back of a spoon so that they are about 7 cm wide.

5. Fry the latkes over a medium heat for about 4–5 minutes on each side, or until they are golden brown and crisp. Turn them carefully with a spatula and a fork.

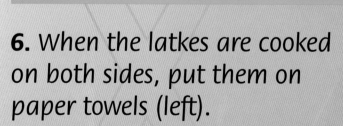

6. When the latkes are cooked on both sides, put them on paper towels (left).

7. Serve your latkes hot with apple sauce, sour cream or sugar.

Glossary

ancient Israel The country of Israel, long ago. Jewish people came from this country.

bagel A hard bread roll shaped like a ring.

blessing A prayer to thank God for something.

customs Ways of doing things in a community.

dreidel A four-sided spinning top with a Hebrew letter on each side.

falafel A ball made from chickpeas and spices, which is fried as a snack.

gelt Money. Parents give their children real or chocolate gelt at Hanukkah.

Hanukkah A Jewish festival. It can also be spelled Chanukah.

hanukiah (plural: hanukiot) A candle holder with nine branches that is lit during Hanukkah. There are eight branches for the Hanukkah candles and one for the 'helper' candle. The 'helper' candle is used to light the others.

Havdalah The ceremony at nightfall on Saturday to mark the end of Shabbat, the day of rest.

klezmer A popular kind of Jewish music that comes from Europe.

kosher Food that Jewish people are allowed to eat.

Maccabees The Jewish fighters who won back Jerusalem more than 2,000 years ago. They were led by a man called Judah Maccabee.

martial art A kind of self-defence that is practised as a sport.

Middle East The area around the eastern Mediterranean that includes Israel, Iraq, Egypt and Turkey.

oil lamp The lamp with burning oil that was always kept alight in the Jewish Temple.

rabbi a Jewish religious leader.

religion school Saturday or Sunday school at the synagogue, where children learn about Jewish history and the Jewish religion. They also learn Hebrew, the religious language of the Jews.

Shabbat The Jewish day of rest. It lasts from just before sunset on Friday until it is dark on Saturday evening.

synagogue The place where Jewish people meet, pray and study.

Temple The main place where Jewish people worshipped more than 2,000 years ago (from 1000 BCE to 70 CE). It was in Jerusalem.

Yiddish A language that has been spoken by Jewish people from northern and eastern Europe for many centuries.

Finding out more

Books

Celebrate Hanukkah With Lights, Latkes, and Dreidels by Deborah Heiligman (National Geographic Books, 2006)

The Hanukkah Family Treasury by Steven Zorn (Running Press, 2004)

Holiday Stories: The Hanukkah Story by Anita Ganeri (Smart Apple Media, 2004)

Holidays, Festivals and Celebrations: Hanukkah by Trudi Strain Trueit (Child's World, 2007)

The Story of Hanukkah by Susanna Davidson (Usborne Books, 2007)

Why Is This Festival Special: Hanukkah by Jillian Powell (Franklin Watts, 2009)

CD-Rom

Our Places of Worship, produced by Wayland.

This CD-Rom explores six major religions found in Britain. Each religion is introduced by a child who follows the faith.

Websites

http://judaism.about.com/od/chanukah/a/hanukkahkids.htm

This website provides links to Hanukkah activities for children.

http://judaism.about.com/od/chanukahrecipes/Hanukkah_Recipes.htm

This website provides links to Hanukkah recipes.

http://www.bbc.co.uk/schools/religion/judaism/hanukkah.shtml

The BBC schools website about Hanukkah, also contains weblinks.

http://www.open-sez-mefestivals.co.uk/hanukkah.htm

This website contains basic information about Hanukkah.

http://www.ort.org/ort/edu/festivals/hanukkah/index.html

This website explains the history and customs of Hanukkah, plus songs and the dreidel game.

Note to parents and teachers: Every effort has been made by the Publishers to ensure that these websites are suitable for children, that they are of the highest educational value, and that they contain no inappropriate or offensive material. However, because of the nature of the Internet, it is impossible to guarantee that the contents of these sites will not be altered. We strongly advise that Internet access is supervised by a responsible adult.

Index